POLAND

poems by

Kurt Steinwand

Finishing Line Press
Georgetown, Kentucky

POLAND

This book is dedicated to my mother-in-law, who as a young girl had lived through the invasion of Poland by the Nazis, their occupation, and the subsequent Russian takeover.

Copyright © 2020 by Kurt Steinwand
ISBN 978-1-64662-158-3 First Edition
All rights reserved under International and Pan-American Copyright Conventions. No part of this book may be reproduced in any manner whatsoever without written permission from the publisher, except in the case of brief quotations embodied in critical articles and reviews.

ACKNOWLEDGMENTS

"Occupation" first appeared in *New Millennium Writings*.

Front cover image: Star-of-David armband. Item from the collection at the National Holocaust Centre and Museum, Nottinghamshire, UK. Image used with permission. The museum describes the image as follows: "Hans Frank, Governor General of Nazi occupied Poland, decreed on November 23rd, 1939, that all Jewish people over a certain age had to wear a 4-inch-wide white armband displaying a blue Star of David on their right arm. The intention was to isolate, harass and humiliate people, and further embedded Nazi ideology that Jewish people were different from everyone else by marking them out from the rest of the population."

Thank you to Erica Dawson and Alan Michael Parker for reviewing this collection, and to Sophia Christman for translations.

Publisher: Leah Maines
Editor: Christen Kincaid
Cover Art: National Holocaust Centre and Museum, Nottinghamshire, UK
Author Photo: Yvonne Steinwand
Cover Design: Elizabeth Maines McCleavy

Printed in the USA on acid-free paper.
Order online: www.finishinglinepress.com
    also available on amazon.com

Author inquiries and mail orders:
Finishing Line Press
P. O. Box 1626
Georgetown, Kentucky 40324
U. S. A.

Table of Contents

End and Begin —*Szymborska* 2

I
Diary *13.02.40* 4
Wrzesień September 1939 5
Stukas Made of Sticks 6
The Unchosen 7
Peace Is Obsolete 8
Death's Head 9
Bullet Rain *in the Generalgouvernement* 10

II
Diary *21.04.41* 12
Occupation 13
Arrival *Auschwitz* 16
Shoes *Majdanek* 17
Hothouse *Treblinka* 18
Katyń Massacre 19
Horses of the Białowieża 20

III
Diary *15.06.44* 22
Lipiec July 1944 23
Reconquered 25
Immigrants 26
Israel 27
You Will Say No More 28
The Polish Way 29

Epilogue 30

Flame Maple —*Violins of Hope* 31

Notes 32

Polish Translations 34

Map attribution: Dennis Nilsson. Licensed under the Creative Commons Attribution 3.0 Unported (https://creativecommons.org/licenses/by/3.0/deed.en) license.

End and Begin   —*Szymborska*

A Jew escaped, hid in the forest,
slipped from farm to farm,
slept under piles of filthy hay.

His brethren got collected,
so many netted pigeons,
punished for their community
in a plot to erase an entire race.

He took pot shots at patrols,
ran like a buck to a hideout
shared with pigs and peasants.
The Reich choked on Europe's bones,
gluttons for gems, Old Master nudes.

Purge and devour, he daydreamed.
May fat Göring get the gout.
May privates rot from the rape.
Drink our black, ancient curse.

When he heard Hitler had bitten cyanide
he danced a *mazurek*, imagined Russians
skewering the eyes with bayonets,
toasting the body, ripping off limbs,
barbarians to roasted chicken with kraut.

Yet that could not return his village,
his family's imported Steinway stacked in a cave,
played by splayed feet of the *Judenräte*.

I

Diary   13.02.40

My thawing hands barely hold this pencil.
Letters shake as if bombs still strike.
That was September. With a new year
it is trains moaning in to *Lublin Główny*.
The SS lined up along the *plac Dworcowy*
as passenger cars arrived from Kraków. Cold makes
everything breakable. Who are these masses?
Some roamed the square until they dropped.
Soldiers shot in the air if we moved too close.
A group in black uniform waved for our cart,
but we turned a corner, left the city, back to our village
nested in snow-blank hills. The fireplace purrs.
I am glad for home, sorry for those lost in winter.

Wrzesień   September 1939

Fanned by wind from the west
a child surmounts a hill,
one of many in a rumpled landscape,
glacier-pressed to form the Polish Plain.
A dearth of mountains to slow conquerors
until the Carpathians in the south.

Strata under centuries, the country
changes status, gets bartered,
sliced, divided like so much kielbasa.
Its people remain. This young lass
endures, weeps paths clean again
where straggler sheep ramble across.

At the crest, this child sees along the horizon
dark shapes casting long, moving shadows,
rising dust the wind pulls like wool.
A rumble. Does she feel the ground trumble?
Mój Boże. She drops her rye loaves.
They roll into the sand, ruined.

Stukas Made of Sticks

She knew they were coming.
Cavalry met them at the border
and were annihilated
by Panzers, great grinding machines
straight out of Brothers Grimm,
black crosses stenciled on their sides.
Not the Christian ones.
In distant Warszawa, shelling
was volcanic, surreal.

Within the month they leaned at her porch,
smoking Eckstein cigarettes.
They entered her school in shiny black boots.
An officer lifted her into his arms,
held her like his own private sock doll.
She was tiny for her age.
He took her for a toddler since she refused to speak.
She was pinched by his insignias
as he casually ordered a building blown up.

Instead of dolls she played with sticks tied
to make Stukas. Acorns were bombs.
They built towers, monitored her childhood.
She hid her country's history books.
An uncle, caught with the partisans,
was gunned down on September's last day.
Like locusts the Luftwaffe buzzed the sky.
Emblazoned with pagan symbols
they crisscrossed Heaven, dark as blasphemy.

The Unchosen

It was so long ago, she explains,
but something more:
reluctance, pain. Of watching
lives taken like boot-crushed bugs,
but more.

Of having to proffer gratitude
when she'd rather see those goose-steppers
strewn like the red of corn poppies
on the road to her ancestral home.

To smile when she feels tears,
unable to act on such horror, an act,
all actors getting fed their lines (food is key)
in epic parody of world deprivation.

Of claiming hatred against one another
when neighbors did nothing to antagonize,
and in plentiful times traded eggs
for beef, butter for bread, each farm's sustenance,
and gave little thought to religion.

To wish another's demise
so she and her kin may keep on existing.
To stay mute as they're marched away,
then say good riddance and spit in the dirt
where they'll get buried, unmarked,

when she means just the opposite
and means no harm, but war is affliction,
affiliations, condemnation,
blind acceptance to escape
that bare, unbearable weight.

Peace Is Obsolete

Ona jest żydówka,
the small old woman shouts,
dragged from the butcher,
heels scraping the floor.

Żydówka, she points with fury,
attempting in her broken German,
Take her, too! She is Juden.

In perfect Polish, holding a clipboard,
the *Oberwachmeister* asks
the one who is left,
Tell me, do you believe in Christ?

Tak, she says, *He sends angels in tanks to save us.*
The officer smacks his clipboard, laughs,
*Ja, there are claims of the Second Coming,
but,* he warns, *the slouching one from that Irish poet.*

He sighs, *Your land is conquered enough.
This is the Flood, the endgame,
check and mate. Do you play chess, Frau?*

*Tak, I play everything.
I love Germans, the Wehrmacht,
Wagner, Oktoberfest, Kris Kringle.*

*You state you are Catholic [check],
vow allegiance to your Savior [check].
These answers allow you to live,
and what is the sin in wanting to live?*

A penetrating smile.
Armored horses.
Peaceful shoulders, hips of hills.
She lies to live.

Death's Head

At the school the *Rottenführer*
simply appears one day like a gypsy,
struts cock-proud in uniform
as though in charge from the beginning.
He tells administration to carry on,
waves his gloves as if clearing dust.

But teachers start to disappear,
one, then another.
The officer bounces a girl
on his offensive knee.
She protests, and he latches to her arm,
the look from his insulted face
meant for imminent reprise.

Instead, a surprise—he gives a gift,
a totenkopf ring, skull and thigh bones
she doesn't tell her father about,
nor the bruising hold, nor the horsey ride

as he frets about how to feed soldiers
with his modest farm, and his neighbor's.
They talk at the dinner table
about stormtroopers who've moved in;
three in the barn, more arriving.
They calculate while she wears the ring,
her arm in salute to no one.

Bullet Rain *in the Generalgouvernement*

Lightning, men lighting pipes
in dark curtained rooms,
spark then latent phosphor thunder.
In cities, Warszawa and Kraków, people die,
or are they all really just numbers?

Alarms of an angry God, a furious leader—
every oven blast a casualty.
Drops, one by one on sand outside her room
late at night, flashes and rumbles.
Water collects, gains rhythm like a Jewish musical

in Lublin, like polka, faster, frantic.
Someone is tapping on her window.
Friend or foe, she doesn't know anymore.
Monsters emerge from under her bed and dance
with armbands, epaulets, killing machines.

They take her childhood, throw it into a bullet rain.
In these times she feels the land, her motherland,
should flood and right itself. Monsters will succumb,
leaving flowers and bees and sun.
But the rain falls with insistence, angry

the way that man gives speeches she's watched
on newsreels at the Panteon, the man spitting gibberish,
pounding his podium, punching at invisible heads.
She wonders what it means to get liquidated,
clutches her Marzanna doll to drown in Spring.

II

Diary   21.07.41

Today our conquerors started a camp,
a prison of sorts for the Russians they captured.
The East has exploded, match to spilled fuel.
A flock of waxwings took over our cherry trees.
They popped each fruit with strong beaks
as local jays bombarded from above.
Leaves shook as the bandits cloistered within,
filling their bellies, getting drunk off the juice.
The jays battled bravely, squawked in protest.
In an instant the intruders scattered, erupting
out of branches into war-grey sky. Our birds
gave short chase, returning in triumph,
so there is hope for the trees, deep, impervious.

Occupation

Factory gate.
The sergeant-major at a foldable table
wears a swastika on his arm.
A civil servant with the same symbol
holds a stack of papers that flutter
like doves taking wing.
Not by wind, but trucks rumbling past
and air sucked up, following.
Exhaustion. Citizens look gassed.

Occupation? The man is careful
not to say artist or teacher.
Draftsman, he says with Polish pride.
I can draw battlefields, these city streets.
The sergeant-major over his shoulder: *Zeichner,*
and it is written into the doves.

Occupation? The man pushes up
a teenager in a wheelchair. *Smile,* he whispers,
and the young man shows all teeth and gums.
This is my son. He is a timekeeper.
Accurate to the second. Go ahead, test him.

The sergeant-major stares back.
The father trips on his own tongue:
…and dishwasher. Goes all day. Never chafes.
The sergeant-major over his shoulder: *Geschirrspüler,*
as the other holds tightly to the doves.

That's right. The father points at the papers,
'Gesher-spooler'. Write it down.
He imitates writing, stamping.

Can the child speak for himself?
Of course. Excuse me. Speak, my boy.
I mean, young man. You're nearly a man,

so the son asks, *What kind of car do you drive?*
The two men look at each other
as doves blow wild, trying to break free.

We drive Mercedes, says the sergeant-major
with a snort as he stamps one of the books,
hands it back. Laughter, such a strange echo
among exhaust and din of the city.

They follow two soldiers shouldering rifles.
The sergeant-major calls after them:

I hope you like trucks. More laughter.
We have many. And more tanks on the way!
A pigeon flock explodes from a ledge.

A soldier blocks the father with his rifle.
The other takes over pushing his son
along the dirt lot where trucks idle,
mufflers like in a cabaret full of smokers.

He rolls further into the distance.
Mist diffuses. Engines rev. Gears catch.
A ringing fills the man's ears.

I'll be right there, my boy, he shouts.

What is this? he asks, confronting the soldier.
That's my son. He relies on me.

With Lugers troops shoot pigeons from the sky.

A ramp is pulled, and the other rolls his boy
into the payload filled with children.
He tilts the chair, shakes it like emptying a sack.
His son falls out, cries in a cold drizzle.

The soldier pushes the empty chair, mud
collected on its wheels, disappears behind a tent.

His boy reaches through the truck's slats,
calls for him. A blur, but it is him.
His father knows the terrified screams,
their legs useless as wings in a cage.

Arrival *Auschwitz*

Ladled out from the eyes of elders,
starsze panie, heads scarved like bandages.
(Where are the fighting-age men?)
They see the end has already passed.
The nameless help each other

down from crowded cars meant
for livestock, reeking of feces,
bodies, sawdust. They are ordered to leave
their possessions along the tracks,
assured they will be reunited.

Where is this hell-forgotten place? Answers vague
as the soot-smeared sky, a reconceived Xanadu.
Khan, the commandant with cold-ember eyes.
Pruned lips proclaim, *These are the worst of times.*

The young rivetted, each contracted pupil
a conception, aborted embryo.
They dare to think an adventure simply misunderstood.
Stars sewn onto jackets, they see they are chosen.
This is a play. They learn their parts. They are stars.

Shoes *Majdanek*

If you've been ordered to remove them,
you're probably dead, not reading this warning.
Crippled, you're dead.
Jew, all of you, and your shoes.
Gypsy, do you wear any? Dead as Dracula.
Dwarf, dead, delivered to the lab.
Twins, double-dead, shoes twice-removed.

Buty, you can't burn them; rubber stinks too much.
The ovens are backed up, anyway.
Drop your watch onto that pile, jewelry over there.
Leave your fillings on this table. Need a dentist?
You're in luck. Keep your socks dry, your feet from rot.
The pink pair of a ballerina, boil them for soup.
Feet wear the fates of civilizations.

Hothouse   *Treblinka*

A room full of plants to beautify the gas chamber.
My job is to load the healthiest onto pallets.
I'm the only one working; the rest lie around.
Someone's eaten the flowers, started on the leaves.
I wouldn't, a countryman says. *They may be poison.*

Someone else—not me, I protest, to no response.
Hell to pay. I'm pricked by a blackberry, suck the blood.
When do we eat? I can't think straight without a snack.
The countryman says, *Take it easy. Here, try these on,*
tosses me a striped top and matching bottoms.

They smell of manure, but I put them on, realizing I'm naked.
Someone's shaved me, and I want my hair back
to put in my food bowl, make a salad. *I need dressing.*
Russian. Another wakens who speaks my language:
We eat when they call us. Now shut your big mouth.

But where do I sleep? I'm tired, and no one helps.
He jabs toward a neatly-made four-poster, clean pillows.
Now that's more like it, I declare, but as I lay there
the bed is a splintery pallet with more above and below,
like a nursery and we're the plants on sale.

I hope to grow toxic berries to serve the guards.
I fall to sleep, head on the flip-side of my bowl.
A man groans. In a dream he vomits, so I can eat.
I dream the flora is ready for burial,
buds blooming. Then the door bursts open.

Schnell! Schnell! They dig a gun into my ribs
that I dream are barbequed, basted in sauce.
Poked with a fork, I'm done. It's my turn
to slake my thirst, to walk into the stabbing light
and tell them this is all a mistake.   *Mmmm, steak.*

Katyń Massacre

We were no match for their firepower.
As men and officers we accept our surrenders.
We march into deep forest where animals
run from us. Uniformed beasts remain,
desensitized to killing. We know our fates,
the marching dead, our wives already widows.
War inflicts the finest details

such as morning glories plowed aside,
an entire ecology of blue flowers roiled
like playful boys into soil. Unnatural trench
crossed with tracks and shovel marks,
otherwise crisp, fragrant air doused in diesel.
High in fir trees a murder of crows.

What am I doing in this ditch?
We stand among the sweat-stink of comrades,
many who sob, hands tied behind them,
unbecoming an officer. I will die in my boots,
muddied yet dignified, in regulation.

German efficiency, Polish cleanliness.
I think of my wife dusting the house, her body
stretched to reach the higher shelves
of our good china, knickknacks collected
over our marriage. My breath catches.
We would have had children.

When bulldozers leave
and the ground is raked, strewn again with leaves,
and sporadic quiet of the forest returns, no one will know
why the ground there turned so fertile,
flesh-fed, uniforms soaked with absolution.

Horses of the Białowieża

In the last virgin forest
scientists take the best specimens back to Berlin.
Starving citizens break into the zoos
and eat the animals.
On the Eastern Front soldiers shoot them,
swallow meat raw as the Red Army swarms,
hack with bayonets into dun-colored hide.

In the last virgin forest
Europe hunts the pure breed toward extinction.
Nazis, in haste, leave some alive.
Russians, overrunning, leave some, too.
From these few elusive survivors
a new population is born
like Jews, gypsies, the innocents.

III

Diary   23.07.44

This morning we watched a plane with a red star
on its tail dogfight with a Messerschmitt.
We like ones that have a shark's mouth
painted on their noses. Father said the fighter we saw
might be American, but I claimed it for Russia.
On the ground, Germans scurried in general panic.
All day we heard dull drumbeats. The plane whined
as it pulled out of a dive, pursued with skill.
The pilot ejected, cartwheeled, then hung from a silk cloud.
A crash.   After weeklong rain, mosquitoes hatched.
They drink from my eyes, accost my ears. I swat,
smearing red on my arm; his blood, my own.

Lipiec   July 1944

Down from Kamionka my father
drives our konik and cart to the city's edge
where watchtowers and chimneys
of the camp come into view. Smoke,
streets with rubble piled like buildings had stopped
mid-construction, or demolition.

A few citizens wander the square.
Three horses with bridles, reins dragging,
trot rider-less along *Krakowskie Przedmieście*
as though window-shopping.
The arms factory silent this morning.
Swastikas hang from lampposts.

The camp gate is half-open. No guards. No SS.
We stop the wagon heaped with vegetables
from our farm. Officers would take choice produce
for their private meals, leave the rest
to go into pots to make a simple soup for prisoners.
This time, no one is at the gate.

We are watching a pile of clothes smolder
when a shaved head peeks out of a building,
then another, with sunken eyes squinting
at the sun. They sniff at the charred wood.
Long, bony fingers grasp the door's edge.
From the east some muffled gunfire,

familiar deep rumble of tanks;
loose, clanking gears grinding on grease.
One of the bodies is out, stares at the vegetables,
not quite human, but upright. Another sniffs
in stained striped pajamas. More emerge
from the long line of wooden buildings.

They head for the gate with unsure steps.
The watchtowers have no eyes. Barbed wire
drips with dew like spun spider webs.
A crow caws, answered by its brother.
We, mere peasants, dismount, speechless.
I feed our horse a head of lettuce.

Shaved skulls gather at the fence,
not daring to walk through the gate.
From the Front the sounds get clearer,
of cogs turning within each other,
chattering like winter teeth, vital dead metal,
the appearance of life in a murdered country.

Reconquered

The Russians barge in and search cupboards,
demanding food, liquor, shouting like addicts.
Two climb the attic ladder, dust powdering our table.
Others chew on bones of our eaten lunch.

Here is Warszawa vodka. The best. Take what you like.

Dirty soldiers press chapped lips to bottles.
Dirty soldiers lay on beds with filthy boots on.
Mother yells, swats at them with her broom.
Mother, the chickens escaped, squawk in outrage.

Gunfire. They're killing our livestock.
The army marches through our field like bull ants,
crops ransacked. One who speaks our language
says they want to kill Nazis for Stalingrad.

Where are the damn Germans?
They left days ago, like animals sensing fire.
The town burns, homes searched.
Streets bleed red for want of revenge.

Immigrants

In Pittsburgh the newlyweds buy a new Ford Fairlane.
The husband shakes hands with the dealership's owner.

Sofia, come here, he calls, *this gentleman is Polish.*

She appears from around a Vote for Kennedy poster
on an easel in the showroom, offers her hand.
Miło cię poznać, the owner says, nodding, grinning.
His sleeves are rolled up, exposing a blurry number tattoo.
He notices her stare. *I am from Będzin.* She stares.
They moved me to Auschwitz. She stares at the digits.

*Talent kept me alive. I repaired their Volkswagens.
I was a kid but had a skill my father taught me.*
He grins to mask emotions. *They gassed my parents
and kept me alive. I was liberated by the Reds.
I was all that was left of my family.*

All the while he grins, as though grateful to have lived,
as if that kind of luck was a normal course in life.
I met my God, he says, *and he gave me a number.
Unreadable now. I have it memorized, but I will not tell.*
He laughs. *Instead, I have a name. People are not numbers.*

No, no, they sure aren't, the husband agrees.

Sofia is scornful. *You were the reason for that mess,* she says,
your greedy Jew fingers. She spits onto the showroom tile,
walks away back around the Kennedy poster.
He reaches into his pants pocket, unfolds a handkerchief,
carefully wipes the spot clean from his floor.

Sorry about that, the husband says. *She hates the war, not you.
Here, take the keys. I won't blame you for not wanting our business.*

The owner waves the handkerchief dismissively, behind his grin.
Nie. Enjoy your car, and may your marriage be a blessing.

Israel

Many who escaped the butchery
flow like on streams coalescing in a desert
beside a violet sea, barren yet redeemable land
with cypress shaped like candle flames
burning blue-green, casting cool shade.
Is this a homeland? Here, home of Abraham,
prophets, and saviors. In the desert

they find an oasis but are forced to build walls
to grace it. *Again, is this a homeland?*
More flow in human rivers, declare their sovereignty.
Armies guard, bombs explode, mosques murmur,
synagogues welcome the dispossessed, churches sanctify lambs
that avoided slaughter. Mother calls over the wall.
Father breaks bread for the kingdom to come.

You Will Say No More

Won't answer the door,
feel you've already said too much,
that some current dictator
will come for you in your traitorous talk.

Your favorite phrase, *worse than the Nazis,*
out of context like your country possessed.
And how can any destructive mind
superior or inferior, claim an adequate rationale?
Cryptically: *One does what one must to survive.*

Your own voivodeship was Germanized,
was to serve the Aryans as a purified paradise.

With you the cataclysm lives on in frailty
like candles and their sputtering wicks.
Even those brief, innocuous sparks remind you
of incendiary bombs of a botched experiment,
never to reveal in full.

The Polish Way

For holding the tongue when accused,
mute to blizzard and blitzkrieg,
a shrug for the rising flood.
They have seen it all,
in the wrong place and time, so easily taken,
too flat to defend the Bloodlands.

For working hands precisely
when the unskilled insist on speed.
For a little *bigos*, then rest, chin to chest.
Everyone has grown. Everyone is old.
They know. They remember the Winged Hussars
and brave cavalry charges,

but choose to end the oral tradition
rather than continue to suffer.
Could more have been done?
Who is to judge? To say merely, *It was bad,*
and no one but the Children of War
knows what terror that means.

Epilogue

My look was different from theirs.
They gathered between classes, shadows
that caught me. *Albino*, they ridiculed,
holding my gaze while one
crept behind, tore out a fist of cottony hair
shown in triumph as the rest cheered.

This is how it starts
for the Wussy, Albino, Jew Boy
(these names, and more).
The condemnation, merciless heritage,
and parents with approving nods
preserve the way it's always been.

No one wants to be alone.
Everyone needs a clan, a protectorate.
Is it that simple?

Is reasoning in my skin, my clothes, my friends?
Possessions, connections to where it begins *(mother?)*,
assurance in the same love, the same songs
from prejudice boxed and carried wherever we go.

Flame Maple   —*Violins of Hope*

Whether brain
or body,
no one can enslave
a beauty to the ear,
delicate waves
in thin voice, choice wood
brought alive
by well-wrought fingers,
a language without time
or place,
its own vibrant,
colorful race.

Notes

In order of appearance (source: wikipedia.com):

Wisława Szymborska: Polish poet who wrote "The End and the Beginning" about the aftermath of war

Hermann Göring: one of the most powerful officers in the Nazi Party

mazurek: lively Polish folk dance in triple meter

Judenräte: "Jewish council"—World War II Jewish-German-collaborative administrative agency imposed by Germany, principally within the ghettos of occupied Europe

Septmember 1, 1939: Germany invaded Poland. Two days later, Britain and France declared war on Germany

SS: The Schutzstaffel, under Heinrich Himmler, the foremost agency of security, surveillance, and terror in Germany and German-occupied Europe

Carpathians: mountain range in central and eastern Europe that skirts the southern border of Poland, which is a country of mostly low hills

Stuka: Junkers Ju 87—German dive bomber during World War II

Oberwachmeister: a senior rank in the German army

Wehrmacht: the unified armed forces of Nazi Germany

that Irish poet: William Butler Yeats

Death's Head (totenkopf): skull and crossbones insignia used by the German military before and during World War II, notably used by the division of the SS that ran concentration camps and death camps

Generalgouvernement: German zone of occupation after the joint invasion of Poland by Nazi Germany and the Soviet Union in 1939

Lublin: major city in eastern Poland where nearly all of its Jewish population was murdered during the Holocaust

Marzanna: doll that is used to celebrate the end of winter by performing a folk rite in which it is either set on fire or drowned in a river, or both

Xanadu: mythical paradise from the poem, "Kubla Khan", by Samuel Taylor Coleridge

Auschwitz, Majdanek, Trebkinka: Nazi concentration camps and death camps located in Poland, Majdanek within sight of the city of Lublin

Katyń Forest: in western Russia, site of a mass murder of Polish officers in 1940

Białowieża Forest: claimed to be a former habitat of the extinct tarpan, a subspecies of wild horse

Messerschmitt BF 109: German World War II fighter aircraft that was the backbone of the Luftwaffe (the German air force during the war)

konik: Polish primitive horse—small horse originating in Poland

Russians: liberated Majdanek on July 23, 1944

Vote for Kennedy poster: John F. Kennedy, who ran for president in 1960

Będzin: city in western Poland that had a vibrant Jewish population until World War II, when the Nazis established a Jewish ghetto there

Violins of Hope: a collection of Holocaust-related instruments in Tel Aviv, Israel, restored by master violin maker Amnon Weinstein and his son Avshalom

Polish translations, in order of appearance:

główny: central (train station)
plac: plaza
Wrzesień: September
Mój Boże: My God
Ona jest żydówka: She is a Jewish woman
tak: yes
starsze panie: older ladies
buty: shoes
Lipiec: July
Miło cię poznać: It's nice to meet you
nie: no
bigos: traditional Polish food with cabbage or sauerkraut

Kurt Steinwand is a writer, artist, and teacher. He holds an MFA from the University of Tampa, and his poetry has appeared in numerous journals including *The Cincinnati Review, Gargoyle, New Millennium Writings,* and *Poet Lore.* He teaches students who have special needs, at a middle school in the Tampa Bay area, where he lives with his wife, Yvonne, and son, Dylan. Their son, who has muscular dystrophy, has inspired him to be an advocate for people who have handicaps, to teach in the field of Exceptional Education (disavowing a career in advertising), to run marathons for charities such as Parent Project Muscular Dystrophy, and to write, yes, even when the answers seem to always be, 'no.'

"Of *Poland,*" the author explains, "my mother-in-law allowed two interviews before claiming that was all she remembered of her time as a child in occupied Poland. She was six when Hitler invaded, eleven by the time Russia chased out the Nazis. She offered no photographs, no documentation or ephemera, just a few hesitant words. Then she wished to take back what little she said, the guilt of that time and place still dominant. What she refused to say was as poignant as what she did say. In a single month I wrote a first draft, editing for a year afterwards. These poems started as slivers, brief anecdotes, and that's how they exist. There's nothing complete about this thin book, nor fully resolved about the war itself. When those who witnessed all die out, the slivers can remain, something someone held, someone or thing perhaps freed."

www.ingramcontent.com/pod-product-compliance
Lightning Source LLC
LaVergne TN
LVHW040117080426
835507LV00041B/1275